Mind the Business

Mind the Business

Mastering Management and Partnership Principles for Success

Henry Strive

Copyright © 2024 Henry Strive

All rights are reserved. No part of this book may be copied, stored, or transmitted in any form or by any means, whether electronic, mechanical, photocopying, recording, scanning, or otherwise, without the publisher's prior written consent.

This book is nonfiction. Names, personalities, businesses, locations, events, and occurrences are either invented by the author or utilized fictitiously. Any similarity to real people, alive or dead, or genuine events is entirely coincidental.

Table of Contents

Introduction..5
Unveiling the Essence of Business Acumen 5
Chapter One...6
Know Your Partner (Part 1)...6
Chapter Two 10
Know Your Partner (Part 2)...10
Chapter Three 14
Know Your Partner (Part 3)...14
Chapter Four 17
Holding Regular Meetings With Your Partners Is Very Important. (Part 4) 17
Chapter Five..26
Partnerships. (Part 5): We must always, always respect agreements, and contracts..26
Chapter Six 33
All "Subject to Change" 33
Chapter Seven...36
How do you turn a small business into a big business 36
Chapter Eight..41
First Things First: Get Organised 41
Chapter Nine:..45
How do you turn a small business into a big business?.....45
Chapter Ten 47

Management is the X-factor 47

Chapter Eleven...57

Being Business-Mined (Part 1)...57

Chapter Twelve...60

Being Business-Mined (Part 2)...60

Chapter Thirteen 63

Being Business Minded (Part 3).......................................63

Change is coming to your Business! 63

Chapter Fourteen 65

Being Business Minded (Part 4).......................................65

Chapter Fifteen 68

Being Business Minded (Part 5).......................................68

"Witty inventions" 68

Chapter Sixteen..72

Being Business Minded: So who is making the money? (Part 6) 72

Conclusion 76

Embracing the Dynamics of Change 76

Introduction

Unveiling the Essence of Business Acumen

In the dynamic world of business and industry, success depends not only on goods or services but also on the ability to recognize and negotiate changing paradigms. "Mind the Business," a book, explores the fundamental ideas that characterize successful entrepreneurship and adaptability to change.

You will read stories in each of its chapters that shed light on critical junctures in the history of business—junctures where bold thinking and quick thinking have transformed sectors and elevated people to previously unheard-of heights. Every tale, from the revolutionary introduction of smartphones to the game-changing effects of mobile money services, demonstrates the strength of intelligence, flexibility, and foresight.

Chapter One

Know Your Partner (Part 1)

It was the first time I met a billionaire! I had travelled all the way to Houston, Texas, my first visit to America. Time and space constrain me from telling you what I had gone to see him about.

I planned to be there for a week.

The first day, he invited me to lunch. And every time I tried to talk about the business idea, he would brush me aside and say, "Tomorrow, son." The next day, I managed to see him, but only for a few minutes. And when I tried to raise my business plan, he said, "Tomorrow, son," then changed the subject, asking instead, "What do you think of Houston?" ...and again invited me for dinner, this time with his wife. On the third day, he invited me to his office, stared at me, and finally said, "Son, I like you. The most important thing about business is to know your partner. I like what I have seen of you. Now that I know you a little, you can discuss with my people the details of what you have in mind." And with that, he politely led me out of his office.

Over the next few days, I faced the most intense grilling about my life and background that I had ever faced. They wanted to know everything about me. And that was before they asked a single question about my business idea. I learned later that even in those three days of informal discussions, they had been evaluating me! I did not mind, because this is one of the most important rules of the game, at the very top.

Remember what I said before?

"Every game has its rules and its own language."

This is one of them:

Know your partners.

That encounter with the most successful person in business I had yet met gave me a lifelong lesson:

You must know your partner.

It is not possible to grow big on your own. You will need partners. In the end, it is really all about partnerships.

Many people think that succeeding in business is about having a good idea and then raising capital. If you do not know how to forge meaningful, long-term partnerships based on mutual trust, you will not make it.

Who are your partners?

How well do you really know them?

Incidentally, I never did business with the Texan business executive because my idea was actually not that good, but I learned how to evaluate and to be evaluated; that was priceless!

In looking back at nearly 30 years in business, I have found that whenever something went wrong and I found myself facing difficulties, I could almost always trace my way back to the wrong choice in business partners. As time has gone by, I have increasingly improved how I select the people with whom I will do business.

I could have chosen to share with you some of the most bitter experiences I ever endured at the hands of the wrong partners, but it is not necessary.

There are two lessons for you to take away from this chapter:

First, always strive to conduct yourself in such a way that you can stand the scrutiny if your progress requires thorough evaluation by others. You should avoid hiding any shameful secrets that may embarrass you if they are revealed.

Secondly, learn to evaluate others properly, and if I might add (yes), even prayerfully, don't just rush to join yourself into a lifelong partnership with people you do not really know, simply because you "clicked"; evaluate properly and professionally. If the person is not willing to talk about themselves and give information that helps you get to know them, then you probably should not commit yourself to a lifelong partnership.

Mind the Business

Chapter Two

Know Your Partner (Part 2)

"If you can phone him, don't write; if you can see him, don't phone." An old sage in business told me: "If there is a misunderstanding with your partner, or even the possibility of a misunderstanding on an issue, if you can phone and discuss it, then do not write. And if there is an opportunity to see the person, then don't phone or write to them; go and see them." As I have said before, you cannot get big and successful in business without the ability to forge strong partnerships. The most important thing in business is to "know your partner.". You must understand their character, their strengths, and their weaknesses. You must understand their aspirations and hopes. And even with all this, misunderstandings will emerge, and there may be a possibility of a misunderstanding. The moment this happens, do not fire off an SMS or an email. Look for an opportunity, as soon as possible, to "talk face-to-face." Do it right away. And when you do meet, listen to what the other person has to say first. And finally, remember what the Bible teaches: "You cannot be right and reconciled at the same time."

I once went into a partnership with two close friends, one of whom I had known for a very long time and loved dearly. We each had a third of the shares. One day, we agreed that the business needed more money, but I could not put in my share, which meant I had to be diluted.

My brothers diluted my shares to almost nothing, and I felt very strongly that they had cheated me in the manner in which they did it. I also felt that they did not appreciate my contribution to the success of the business over and above the cash that went into the business.

So there arose a dispute amongst us...

Given the amount of money involved, this is the type of dispute that spills into the courts. I knew I had a strong case.

Instead, I called one of my friends and offered to sell him my shares. When he asked how much I wanted, I asked him just $1, even though I had invested millions into the venture. I did not even tell him that I felt deeply cheated;

I rather focused on the need to preserve our long relationship, reminding him of the great things he had done for me in the past, which were to me much more valuable than some shares in a business. I asked him to see it, rather, as a gift from me.

If I had focused my attention on demonstrating that I was "right," there would have never been a reconciliation of the matter. I chose instead to be "cheated.".

"Why, the very fact of your having lawsuits with one another at all is a defect (a defeat, an evidence of positive moral loss for you). Why not rather let yourselves suffer wrong and be deprived of what is yours? Why not rather be cheated (defrauded and robbed)?" (2Co6:7).

In the parable, that is popularly known as the "Prodigal Son" (Luke 15:11–32),. One of the principle messages that it "teaches" is the biblical tenants of reconciliation.

Imagine if the elder brother, in that story, had been the one to receive his younger brother and not the father:

The elder brother would probably have berated his younger brother to show him how wrong and foolish he was. No doubt the younger brother would sooner have committed suicide than face his elder brother!

You cannot be right and reconciled at the same time.

Even if you have a marital dispute, if you focus on telling your spouse what he or she did wrong against you and showing them why you are "right" and they are "wrong". You will find it hard to be reconciled.

Rather, allow yourself to be "cheated" (if that is the way you see it) and focus your attention on being reconciled (2 Co 6:7). This does not mean you have given up your principles; it means you are wise, like the "Prodigal Son's Father.". There is a time to be right, and there is a time to be reconciled; you choose.

Chapter Three

Know Your Partner (Part 3)

When I was starting out in business, nearly 30 years ago, I was made to believe that the best partners, were those people in powerful positions, who had the ability to open big doors. Being a young entrepreneur, there were many powerful people who offered themselves to be my "sleeping partners, or "godfathers" to whom I could go if I had trouble with anyone in "the system". As many of you are aware, I was not born into a Christian family. I became a Christian by choice when I was already a well-established businessman. It was a deep personal decision, and this is not the platform to discuss that issue. However, having made this decision, I threw myself with total fervor, often reading the Bible back to back, several times a year, as I tried to "come up to speed", with my new-found faith. It was at this time that I came to realise that I had to "play by and succeed by a different set of rules.".... My partnerships had to align with my faith in, and trust in God... I could not and would not have "sleeping partners" in any business that I do. I could not and would not choose partners simply on the basis of their ability to wield influence or to sponsor my activities. Let me tell you, this set me on a collision course everywhere I went, because I was essentially shunning an entire world system. I was despised and mocked for it. Those who were polite called me naive, and others, who were not so kind, said I was a fool. We "lost" many contracts and many business opportunities. Often, we had to walk away from deals that were just "mouth-watering.". More often than not, we were just threatened and kicked out, leaving others to take over what we had started. And when this happened, I just never allowed myself to have regrets about it. One of my great mentors, Bishop Garlington, once said to me, "You are standing in the river of faith, Don't be afraid. You are not going to be swept away, and you are not going under; use your faith to go over." Then he said to me: "Focus on integrity, because one day, you will be the partner of choice for anyone wanting to do business in Africa, the right way..." Do you want a partner? Let me share with you a secret: "The best partner for you, is not some big powerful politician, or someone with a lot of money, or some big international company. The best partner for you is someone just like you who has the passion for entrepreneurship that you have. Who has the skills to compliment what you do best and is willing to work very hard alongside you? It might be a man or a woman, black or white, or even from a different tribe or nationality from you. What is key is to align your values and respect each other's space. Never mind the money, the power, and the influence... Its not a factor.

Chapter Four

Holding Regular Meetings With Your Partners Is Very Important. (Part 4)

Entrepreneurs are generally very busy people, and they spend their time running around trying to sell their products and to make "ends meet" (as they say). Unfortunately, many entrepreneurs consider having formal meetings a waste of time and simply want to get out there and do things. This is not very wise. It does not matter what business you are in or how small it is; it is important to sit down and have proper meetings. And by this, I do not mean "chatting things over, whilst relaxing, over coffee.". I mean you must have scheduled meetings, during working hours, when you sit down with your partners, and and also with your staff to discuss what is going on in your business. .... Always hold such meetings during normal working hours. It serves as a reminder that you consider it to be an integral part of your business. Before you start your discussion, you must agree on what you are going to talk about and select someone to keep a record ("minutes of your meeting"). Before the next meeting, everyone must agree that the record of your previous meeting is the correct one. This is one of the most important disciplines for you to learn if you want to grow and build your business. As I have said before, such meetings are not serious if they do not begin and end with a discussion on the finances. This is the engine and lifeblood of a business. Proper financial reporting is followed by a robust, competent discussion of the figures. When we were very small, I would begin by saying, "Bookkeeper, take us through your report," and now, thirty years later, it is the same: "CFO, pleas take us through your report." Practice to spend most of your time discussing figures, not just exchanging stories. Remember, you are in business now! In your agenda, you must always have agreements on what constitutes your policies as a business. And these you must write down, and jointly sign with your partners. .... "Keeping proper, written records, is key to your success...". Keep the records safe, and always have copies. It is very bad to operate your business in this day and age (someone as educated as you) on verbal agreements! In your discussion, make sure your discuss, sensitive and difficult issues, for example: "- so how much are we going to pay ourselves in salary? What can we afford?"

"- how many shares do we each have in this business? Let's agree; let's sign... This is business now... Aha, aha!" And remember: Pay everyone their due... Including that little cousin, helping to clean the place.... She has dreams too! Aha, aha... That's business now. Pay your taxes as well.

I once took a great idea for a business to a very successful and prominent older businessman who was also very influential. He agreed to back the idea. Whenever I suggested that we write things down, he would be offended, saying, "Don't you trust me?". I insisted that I wanted things in writing, and I managed to get the first couple of meetings, between us, minuted and signed.

After that, it was so difficult to pin him down; he was always "too busy"; sometimes, I had to wait outside his office or even in his car for hours.

The small business we were doing together became spectacularly successful, surprising even him. Soon I began to hear all kinds of rumors about who owned the business, and my share seemed smaller with each rumor!

And I realized it was my partner who was behind these rumors, as he now seemed to be more interested in spending time at the business; "now it was more important."

In time, I produced the agreements and minutes, reminding him of what we had signed together at the beginning. Then I let him buy it and went my way—wealthier and perhaps a little wiser!

... Choose your partners carefully; don't be unequally yoked simply because you are young and your partner has all the money.

...and keep proper, written records about your business and agreements with people. How you do this, is key to successful partnerships.

Davy asks:

Even when you have one worker?

If you have just one worker in your business,. Have the humility and wisdom to sit down regularly with that person and discuss the business. Allow that person to express their opinion on what they are seeing and hearing from customers and suppliers. You will be absolutely amazed at what you will learn that will improve the business.

When deep calls to deep:

"Brother, please pray for me! Things have just not been going all that well in my business lately."

So I prayed for him while he stood quietly with his head bowed.

After the prayer, I said to him, "I suggest you immediately attend to three things:

Go pay all your workers and their arrears, even if it means selling that beautiful car you have.

Go pay your tithes, since you said you were a Christian. Even if it means selling that beautiful home you have.

Go settle your taxes with the government of your country, even if the system is corrupt and unfair in every way.

Bewildered, he looked at me as though he had seen a ghost.

Remember my chapter on the laws of gravity? Aha, aha, ahaaaa!

Its up to you now... Read on, and say nothing.

Let me challenge you to go one better:

You did then what you knew best to do, but when you knew better, you did better."

Maya Angelou.

Now that we "know better", what else can we do "better"?

Let me show you another area:

If you employ a maid, a Gardner or just someone to help with the children whilst you are at work,. Be sure to give them a proper written contract, even if they cannot read or write. In the contract that you draft, be sure that you is fair. Look at the working hours, the periods of rest, and the holidays. Think about the needs of their own families and children.

Now I know, you might say to me, "but everyone does it here this way?" But does not change begin with you and I?

The "little cousin, from the village", the "cleaner" and the "driver". Let's bring dignity to their jobs... Let's pay them their dues.

It is not right before our God to say, 'I am feeding them, so that is enough.' And then expect your own prayers to be answered when you have a challenge.

And if you are a believer, perhaps you might just find "a smooth flow in the reply to your own prayers."

Winger Writes:

Assist me with a sample contract form for watchman and ground laborers.

I only wish I had the time to draft something that you could use. Perhaps some of our legal friends could do something for you if you gave them your contact information.

However, let me give you a simple piece of advice:

A contract does not have to be a complicated document full of "legalization". All you need is to write a letter to the employee (one or two pages) in which you simply thank them for accepting to work for you as a Watchman (Security Guard), gardner, or cleaner. And then stating what you have agreed to pay them by way of salary. Also leave days, rest periods etc. If you yourself are employed professionally and have a contract, you will already know what should be in a contract.

When you have completed the letter, sit down with the employee and go through it carefully, watching carefully their reaction, ensuring that their fear of you does not just result in agreement, even when they are not happy. If possible, invite someone else to be in attendance as a witness.

Make sure that it is not the type of letter that would make you ashamed one day because you took advantage of someone's desperation or ignorance.

Then the two of you sign, and you give them a copy.

Now the most important thing:

Always, always respect what you have agreed to do. Don't try and get out of it when things get tough.

Chapter Five

Partnerships. (Part 5): We must always, always respect agreements, and contracts

In the book of Joshua, there is a story about a group of people, called the Gibeonites, who managed to secure an agreement with Joshua and his leadership team by false pretences. When the leadership of the Israelites discovered what had happened, they were furious. The intriguing thing is what happened next: Joshua 9:18–20 (Living Bible, The TLB) 18. The people of Israel were angry with their leaders because of the peace treaty. 19 But the leaders replied,We have sworn before the Lord God of Israel that we will not touch them, and we won't. We must let them live, for if we break our oath, the wrath of Jehovah will be upon us." "These things were written, for our learning"; so what do you learn from this incident, that can be of help to you, in your business, even today?

1. Before you enter into agreements of any kind to work with other people, you must do your due diligence of those people properly. However, once you enter into an

agreement and give your word, you must adhere to the agreement that you signed! All too often, people try to back out of agreements they have made if they find that they believe they were misled or the other party did not give them the right information about themselves or even misled them.

2. Adhering to and respecting an agreement with a party that you consider weaker than yourself is the ultimate test of integrity. It is never about the integrity of the other party. It is about your integrity that you must focus on. There is nothing that disturbs me more than business people who do not want to respect agreements they have made when the situation no longer seems to favor them. They are people who default on loan agreements, supply agreements, and contracts simply because they consider the other party too weak to do anything to them. Joshua's integrity was tested to the full when the Gibeonites were attacked and appealed for his help under the agreement. Now, many people would have said, "this is God's vengeance against those lying cheats, let them deal with it, themselves"............read on! -Joshua mobilised his army to go out and fight the enemies of the Gibeonites. - And here is another thing, God joined the fight, with

Joshua, to help save the Gibeonites! When you enter into an agreement, whether it be verbal or written, you must respect it. Don't borrow money from people, and when they come looking for their money, you threaten them and tell them to go away. - Don't promise your employees salaries, and promotions, that you will ignore, once you get them to do what you wanted. - Don't strip your partners of their shares, simply because you believe you have more power. Finally, you must also respect agreements that others have made before you came. If you buy a business or property, respect existing agreements and even titles. If you take over management or leadership, respect every agreement made by your predecessors, even if they were not smart agreements, in your opinion. Time constrains me to tell what happened when a King of Israel, hundreds of years later, ignored this very same agreement with the Gibeonites. God loves integrity.

Over the years, I have sometimes found myself in agreements with other parties that, upon reflection, I have realised were not as good as they should be. I never try to implement only those things I like and ignore the rest. This is wrong. I stick to the letter and spirit of the agreement to the best of my ability.

Failing to pay your staff on the due date is a default on an agreement. You should never allow the situation in your business to get to a place where you are in default of any kind on a contract or agreement.

Sometimes, the circumstances are beyond your control, and I have talked about such situations before. Then what you must do is seek to sit down with the other party and renegotiate the "due dates" in your agreement. Don't act unilaterally by simply telling the other party what you have decided. If it is your workers, you cannot pay, sit down with them or their representatives, and discuss the situation.

Also show them that you, as leaders, are also "taking the pain" by, at the same time, adjusting your lifestyles.

Don't drive out with a Mercedes or continue to fly First and Business Class while workers are unpaid.

We once bid for a cell phone license, in which one of the requirements was that we have a local partner, with a

30%. We found a local group, and they told us that they had money to contribute their 30%. We then entered into a written agreement, in which we agreed to all the terms.

We then bid for the license and won it in a public process.

On the date for payment, our partners did not come up with their share of the money and instead demanded that we fund them; otherwise, they would get the government to cancel the license.

What would you have done?

I told them they were in default on our agreement, and I would invoke our right to find another partner. The following day, the minister, then responsible for telecommunications, announced the cancellation of the license.

We hired a team of local lawyers in that country and began a legal battle that took 4 years to resolve. The courts, re-instated the license, and threw out our local partners, for failure to adhere to the provisions of our agreement.

Sara Writes:

Dear Mr. Strive:

My name is Sara, and I am a business woman in Ethiopia. I am also the coordinator of the Business Gate under the Gates Ministry within Beza International Church. We work hard to promote righteousness and justice through businesses. I just heard you are in Addis Ababa for a meeting.

I would be very grateful if I could meet you with some of my brothers and sisters in Beza just so that you inspire and bless us with your presence. Just for few minutes. Please let me know whom to contact locally to facilitate this.

May God bless you and hope to see you.

Sara

Answer:

It is true; I was in your beautiful country!

I was there to chair the African Green Revolution Forum (AGRF). One of the most important meetings on African agricultural developments.

Unfortunately, I have already left Ethiopia.

There were many requests for me to come back soon, even from the Prime Minister, whom I met just before I left. I promised that I would come back.

We have a lot to discuss!

Chapter Six

All "Subject to Change"

Many years ago, I attended an event to honour Jeff Bezos, the founder of Amazon.com. He is one of the most brilliant entrepreneurs of this generation. A truly remarkable man, whom I greatly admire for his work. As he was being interviewed he talked about what had inspired him to develop the "Kindle". It is one of my favourite tech tools, and I carry one everywhere I go. Something he said, really resonated with me: "Let's not forget that a "BOOK" is an invention. It has been one of the most successful inventions of all time, but it is still an invention." How many of us, look at something, like a book, and think to ourselves: "Someone actually invented this." Often when you have a successful invention that has endured a long time, people begin to think, is came off the Ark with Noah. Yes, there was a time, when there was no book. Even the simple classroom, with a school teacher at the front, is an innovation that did not exist, until a few hundred years ago. Someone out there is thinking about, "how can I re-invent this? What innovation can I introduce to come up with a better more efficient, cost effective method?" These are the people who will go on to change the world. Hey, if you can see it, "its subject to change". And you are the one to change it: This is the mindset that makes you an entrepreneur, either for profit, or for non-profit. Jeff and his team at Amazon invented the Kindle, to replace the book, in paper format. They have sold millions, and it has contributed to making Amazon, valued at more than $200bn, in just a few short years.

Paper money (cash) was invented by someone. Yes, those banknotes that you call "money" were invented by someone:

What a great idea!

But even that is subject to change. Things like Ecocash, M-PESA, Alipay, Paypal, credit, and debit cards. These are all inventions that have been replacing "cash".

Within a few years, you will find it strange to carry cash in your pocket or purse.

When we launched our own service, Ecocash, which is available in several African countries, I made it clear that we wanted to "replace paper money".

Hopefully, I will discuss this with you again one day.

Remember what I said, "If you can see it, its subject to change"?

It can be changed. It can be improved. And if you are the one to do it, then you stand to prosper yourself and your organization.

Every day of my life, I am looking for opportunities to change and improve something to make it better, more efficient, and more reliable.

Each one of us has the capacity to develop this mindset. Try it today, take something simple, redesign it, and keep practicing this every day.

Chapter Seven

How do you turn a small business into a big business

Over the last few months, we have talked a lot about entrepreneurship, and I know many of you have been bitten by the entrepreneurship bug, and you are now trying to get something started, or better yet, you have already started something. Others would simply like to see the organisation they work for become bigger and go outside their region or country. Over the next few weeks, I want to address the question: "How do we turn our small business into a big business?" I know you have a big dream and a vision to see your business become a national champion, and then probably a regional champion, until it is a continental champion, and ultimately a global brand with offices around the world. Yes, it is possible, and you can definitely do it. One of the things I have learned in life is to avoid prescribing formulas. And I know many people would like to be given a formula. When I was in engineering school, I learned that people who cram formulas are destined to fail. The ones who succeed are those who grasp principles, from which formulas are derived. I am going to teach you principles, some of which will surprise you. Some of them will challenge what you have been taught or have come to believe. I hope you will have an open mind and, where necessary, the courage to change something. In the table (link below), which I took from Forbes Magazine, is a list of the world's largest companies, based on revenue (not market value). I have chosen this list because of something I want you to see:

1. Some of these companies have an annual turnover that is as large as the GDP of Nigeria, Africa's biggest economy.

2. A company like Walmart, which is owned by an American family, has more than 2 m, employees. "How is it possible to build and manage organisations of that size?" "How"? "How"?

As an exercise, please research and give me a list of the 5 most valuable companies in the world.

You must give a list, including the company and its market value. No need for discussion, just a list.

Torngee writes:

Based on Financial times global 500, Third quarter of 2014: (ALL.FIG IN MILLION USD)

1 Apple Inc. 603,277.4

2 Exxon Mobil. 401,094.1

3 Microsoft 381,959.7

4 Google 361,998.4

5 Berkshire Hathaway, 340,055.0

Reply:

This is the correct answer. I know some of you also got it right. For those who did not, notice that he not only gives his source but also gives the period when the information applies: "Third Quarter 2014". Some people did not check when the information they had was taken, even though they had the right companies.

1. Apple is the most valuable company in the world, with a value of $603 billion, as recorded in the 3rd quarter of this year.

2. Walmart is the largest publicly listed company in the world when measured in terms of revenues. It generates almost $500 billion a year. However, in terms of market value, it is worth about $203 billion and does not make the top 5.

Why does all this matter?

If you are an entrepreneur or work in anything called a business, these are things that should be on your fingertips. Imagine a football fan who does not know who the best players are or what position they play!

This is your game, right? Well, then, know how it is played and who its best players are.

Now, if you really want to impress me, you can go to the "Closing Bell" numbers at the end of today's trading and see how well these companies are currently doing, whether they have held that value, and their positions.

That is for another day. Let's return to our discussion issue:

How do you turn a small business into a big business?

What you should also be realizing by now is that there are a number of recognized ways of assessing how big a business is.

If someone comes up to you and asks, "So how big is your company?" How do you answer this question in a way that shows you know what you are talking about?

In soccer, if I say, "What team does Ronaldo play for?" Would it be okay to say "Manchester United"? Or even the Chicago Bulls?

I can hear someone laughing. But someone will also laugh at you if you give answers to business questions that are either out of date or show you don't even know the game of business.

Chapter Eight

First Things First: Get Organised

When my children were younger, I would sometimes call them at the end of the day and make them write a list of the things they had done since they woke up. The reason I did this was to make them forever conscious of the need to "account for one's time"; time is an incredibly precious commodity. All these things that you want to do are simply not possible if you are not conscious of the need to account for time. When I visited the United States for the very first time in 1991, I wanted to learn as much as I could about what made it a success. This is something I try to do with every country that I visit around the world. If you look carefully, there is always something you can admire and learn from any nation on earth. In studying the lives of America's founding fathers, I came across the "13 Virtues," which one of them, a man named Benjamin Franklin, wrote himself when he was only 20 years old. I wrote them all down in a note book, and one I will always remember is this: Virtue 1: Industry. Lose no time; be always employed in something useful; cut off all unnecessary actions. It really does not matter what your vision in this life is; whether it is "for profit" or for the great welfare of mankind";" you cannot accomplish it if you are not organised. Make it your personal mantra to always try to be organised and efficient. This is at the core of productivity. Even if you are a hard worker, you will get less from yourself if you are not organised and efficient in how you approach things. We have a lot of work to do to get Africa to realise its potential. It's important that this generation approach this work with a sense of urgency. There is so much you can accomplish if you are highly organised, and it is a fundamental building block for organising others. Being organised is not just a declaration of intent; it must be followed by action. And you must invest in those things that make you more organised and efficient as a person. Never be late to a meeting. If you say let's meet at 10am, be there at 10am. And if, on the rare occasion, you are late, say sorry, even if it is to one of your own children.

A few years ago, I coined the phrase "time thief" to refer to people who have no value for the time of others. It is so important to value the time of others, even if they are your subordinates.

Be a leader with a difference; respect the time of others.

One of my young daughters came to me one day and said, "I have decided I will not have braids in my hair anymore. Surprised, I asked, "Why not? You look great in your braids." She looked at me and said, "I'm concerned about the length of time it takes."

"Maybe you should take a book?"

"That's a good idea."

She was clearly thinking about what Old Benjamin Franklin had said: "Cut off all unnecessary actions." She still does braids now and again. The key issue is that she was willing to look at things in her life that she considered inefficient.

Its great to watch a football game on TV. I do it myself, but I will never watch two games in one weekend. I decided long ago, at the beginning of the season, what games I would like to see. For the rest, I just check scores and read about them in the paper. 10 minutes, done. Let's move on.

In the next chapter, we can begin to turn our attention to how you learn to manage an organization and make it grow bigger.

Chapter Nine:

How do you turn a small business into a big business?

Step 1: Study how organizations are built and managed. In my first chapter on this subject, I referred you to a link showing the five largest companies in the world, using the measure of revenue generation. I also showed you that revenue generation is just one of the recognized measures we use to assess the size of a business. I asked the question, How does one build a big company like Walmart, which has a turnover of nearly $500 billion and employs over 2 million employees? This company is bigger than the economies of nearly all African countries and has more workers than many countries! When I started out in business, nearly 30 years ago, one of the first things, I realised was the importance of learning how to build, and manage an organisation. ....No matter how great your business idea, no matter how smart you are, no matter how innovative your idea, no matter how much money you raise: Listen to me: If you do not know how to build and manage an organization, you will either fail or never be able to realise your dream. The difference between those people who are good entrepreneurs, and those who are great entrepreneurs, is the capacity to build and manage an organisation, that is effective, efficient, and innovative, even as it gets bigger and bigger, and bigger. "This is not something that comes to you naturally. It is a skill you have to acquire through study and practice." Whenever a business fails, if the truth be told, this is 90% of the reason for the failure. Unfortunately, many people never even realise that this is their problem. They might even get angry if you suggest that this is the problem. You can only solve a problem when you realise that there is a problem. For those who do not accept that they could have such a problem, this is not for you. I'm talking to people who want to turn their businesses, no matter how small they are today, into big, global companies, like Walmart or Apple.

Chapter Ten

Management is the X-factor

The size of the business that you run is dependent on your capacity to build and manage an organization. We can talk about vision; we can talk about entrepreneurship; we can talk about innovation; we can talk about all those things, and more. But if you cannot manage, it will come to nothing. At best, you will start something, then someone else will see it who really knows how to manage it, and they will go off and make a success of it while you watch. Sometimes, it will seem like you are destined to always be small. Not true.... See those huge organizations we were talking about, like Walmart and Toyota? .....They are big because they have highly skilled managers who know how to build and operate complex organizational structures. Being an entrepreneur, full of great ideas and innovations, is not enough. You have to become a skilled builder and manager of an organization. You have to be able to attract skilled managers who know how to execute the vision you have in a competent and disciplined manner. Years ago, I remember listening to the finance manager of one of our businesses. He was so stressed, always talking about cash flow problems and our problems with creditors. The next day, I called a top recruiter to my office, and I gave them a simple instruction: "Find me the most skilled finance manager, you can find in this country. Bring me a list of the top five. The person must be capable of running a large organization and have had exposure to best practices from a leading international organization." "There is an African lady working at a big international organization in South Africa. She knows the systems of one of the best companies in the world." "Go get her, please!" Within two months of her arrival, we were swimming in cash! Now we could get bigger. If I had left that stressed guy in place, we would have gone bankrupt, even though we had a great business.

Lockcious Asks:

Yes, that's true, sir. My question is, 'Are managers born or made?'

Answer:

Managers are made. A good personality and character makes them better and even greater. You can acquire management skills through study and training.

James writes:

Understanding management is key to taking any business to an unimaginable, wonderful world. For concise learning on management principles and practices, I recommend you go get Peter Drucker's books. He is one of the greatest management thinkers of our time. God bless Africa and Africans.

Answer:

You are so right, James. As a young entrepreneur, I was also a student of men like Peter Drucker. At that time, it was so difficult to get his books, but I still managed to get almost every book that he ever wrote. There are, of course, many other experts in this field, and as you become more conscious of the need to always be looking for opportunities to grow your skills as a manager, you will discover even more people like Drucker.

Management practice is also an ever-improving discipline, and the fact that you read an MBA five years ago does not mean you now know everything. You must continuously push yourself to study and practice new ideas and innovations in the field.

As I prepared to leave Germany 15 years ago, I held several meetings with some of my key staff (from all levels of the organization). Our company there was still very small. They were excited about the vision I had and the potential opportunities for themselves. I told them that there were 5 things I needed them to do:

1. Uphold utmost integrity, even when you do not see me around.

2. Practice excellence.

3. Go back to school, and I offered to reimburse anyone who improved themselves with any professional grade.

4. Learn another language. In this world, it is a shame to say that the only language you know is that of your mother tongue.

5. Respect diversity.

I knew that men and women who were able to achieve these things would be able to help me build a global business. Such people can succeed anywhere.

Question:

Sir, which books (that talk about business, management, and capacity building) would you recommend for me? NB: I am a young man of 16 years who wants to start some sort of business (selling printed T-shirts). Your recommendation would be of great help.

Thank You.

Answer:

It is good that, at 16, you already want to be a great entrepreneur. The most important thing for you right now is to push forward with your education and get as far as you can. We are living in an age when it will become very difficult to succeed at anything if you do not have a good education. This does not mean people who do not have a good education cannot succeed, but it is that much harder. So before you get into the Business Management books, get stuck into things like maths first.

John Writes:

This is a wow, Dr... thanks so much. Management is much more than mere issuance of instructions to a small group of people. It's more of the ability to look deep down into something and be able to understand how our present action/inaction would affect the future of what we do or what we become. One thing is to start, another is to build, grow, and sustain, and the letter centers on the ability to manage innovatively. Thanks again, sir.

Let there be Light!

Answer:

I love this!

Martin Writes:

I just remembered of a very successful entrepreneur. people always came to him to ask for advice on building an enterprise. he would ask, can you make a burger better than McDonald's? and most would reply yes. Then he would ask, can you build a big burger business like mcdonalds? needless to say the answer was no. and he would tell them it was not about making a better burger but a system that could sell hundreds of thousands of burgers a day.

Answer:

That is correct, Martin.

This is the heart of the issue; I'm talking about Martin:

Management, Management, Management!

Its the X-factor!

A guy takes a small hamburger joint and turns into a global business like McDonalds... How?

A guy takes a flea market business...Walmart started as a flee market... And turns it into a global business with sales of $500 billion! If you read the autobiography of Sam Walton, the founder of Walmart, called Made in America... It is so simple to read, but it oozes with management and organizational genius.

Don't think about management in terms of administering the work of others and barking instructions; there is much, much more. Be conscious of it as a hard professional discipline backed by theory and practice.

After Thought No. 1.

The platform that drives something like Uber is just a tool. Imagine that one day, a young African working in America (like my friend from Ethiopia) were to actually sit down with a couple of friends and redesign the platform to provide public transport in Africa. I know that Uber is already in places like Johannesburg. But I'm looking beyond that: I see an Uber-like service could be used to help deal with the nightmare of queues for Kombis (Matatus) or to help rural people get access to transport when they need to get to the city.

Being "business-minded" allows you to see this kind of possibility. And when you do this, don't be surprised if your company is not bigger than MTN or Safaricom. Such a company will be more valuable than all the mining and oil companies in Africa. What are you waiting for?

After Thought 2.

My daughter, who ordered the Uber on my behalf, told me to rush because she did not want to get a "bad rating, from the driver". What do you mean, "bad rating? I thought you were the customer."

"With Uber, the driver gets to rate you as a customer. And you also rate the driver."

"That is an amazing innovation."

"Welcome to the world of Uber." Said my daughter, laughing.

After thought 3.

A friend of mine is a passionate Manchester United supporter, and I was quite surprised when I said to him that I had been reading about them. Then I told him, "They had a record year last year."

"It was our worst season! How can you say they had a record year?!" He said it with astonished indignation.

"You study soccer; I study the "business of business". I said calmly, "Manchester United are listed on the New York Stock Exchange, and their revenues were about £430 million, an increase of almost 20%. It was a record for them. The commercial side of their business did particularly well. They are a pretty good business; even George Soros buys their shares."

If you are a Manchester United supporter, do you know the name of their CEO, the guy who runs the business? Tip: its not Van Gaal. I''m talking about his boss!)

Seeing the business side is being "business-minded". You can train yourself to be business-minded. Who knows, maybe one day you will not just support a team passionately, but you will also turn your knowledge of that team into a way to earn a little money.

Chapter Eleven

Being Business-Mined (Part 1)

One of the fastest-growing businesses in the world today is a company called Uber. For those who do not know what Uber is, it is essentially a mobile app (a computer program using a cell phone), which makes it possible for you to call a "taxi.". Uber does not own any taxis or cars of its own. The app sends a message (similar to an SMS) to the nearest registered but independent Uber driver within your vicinity. The car will usually arrive at your location within 5 minutes. While using one of these services, the owner of the car proudly told me that he was making a lot of money as the service brought him customers. Uber takes a commission and also does the billing. All he has to do is show up. Then the driver, added this: "Uber has no assets, just some computer servers." Seeing that he was a smart entrepreneur, I then engaged him in a wider conversation about business: I asked him so many questions that he finally asked me, "Are you planning to set up a similar business in Africa?" "Not really.... I'm just "BUSINESS MINDED"; I make it my business, to see the business side of any business." I then surprised him by telling him what I already knew about Uber. For instance, I told him that Uber is now valued at more than $40 billion. They are more valuable than Anglo American, which is one of the largest mining companies in the world. Imagine a taxi hailing service that is more valuable than Anglo, which has been around for more than 100 years, employs tens of thousands of people, and controls some of the largest deposits of diamonds, platinum, iron ore, and coal in the whole world. "Do you think that is fair?" The Uber driver asked. "How can a company with no assets be worth more than a mining company that owns De Beers Diamonds or Anglo Platinum?!" Uber has no assets. They do not even own the cell phone network on which their services operate. "Who would have imagined that someone could come along and change a service as simple as getting a taxi?" $40bn. As we neared the end of my journey, I suddenly asked my driver, who incidentally was an African from Ethiopian: "How does Facebook and Twitter make money?" "Through advertising," he shot back. "What does that mean?" I asked laughing. "Not really sure, sir." I laughed some more, and as I got out of his car, I was still laughing. He looked bewildered by my response. Sadly, I did not have a chance to explain to him why I was laughing. He rushed to his next Uber client, and I went my way. Still laughing.

Chapter Twelve

Being Business-Mined (Part 2).

I will never forget the first time we had to deal with Blackberry, when they produced their phone for the first time. "Our business model is quite simple", the sales executive said, to us: "We charge you, $20/customer, per month. And you can charge on top, whatever you want." My Chief Marketing Officer, who was dealing with them, was livid: "That is ridiculous! We have invested billions of dollars to build the network and to get customers. Now you waltz in here and tell us that you will get the lion's share of the revenue from each customer? How can anyone accept such an arrangement?" The blackberry guy smiled and said quietly, "its's take it or leave it." The matter was escalated to me as chairman. I listened quietly to our senior executives, express their frustrations,and indignation: "That means, we will only get about $5, whilst they take $20; is that fair?!" "Why, why can't they just sell us phones like everyone else? Why do they want a revenue share, as though they are the operator?!" "Do it, and do it now." I said it quietly. Then I explained:

"They have the upper hand. They know that they have an iconic product, which our top customers will want. If we do not sign, they can do serious damage to our business by handing this opportunity to a competitor. This game is no longer about building networks; its the guys who can use our networks for their own businesses who will be king from now on. We better learn to do the same, or at least work with them." The position of Blackberry would remain unchallenged until someone came along with a better product, and that was Apple. They were even more aggressive about what they wanted. There was no debate; we all understood by then. Today, Apple is worth more than $600 billion, making it the most valuable company in history—yes, more valuable than any oil company, mining conglomerate, or cell phone company. Being "business-minded" requires you to understand what I call "changing dispensations" when they occur. If you do not understand why Alibaba, an "online flea market," is worth more than any cell phone company or any mining company, you will not be able to play the business game. Now, think about Uber and learn to be business-minded.

Always look for the principle and avoid formulas.

Before I sit down to write a chapter, I spend some time thinking about one or two principles that I would like to convey to you. The stories I tell are not meant to show my own prowess as a businessman; rather, I tell them to you as a way to convey a principle.

So when you have read the chapter and the story, I urge you to sit down and try to "extract" the principles that you can use again and again in your own life or business situation.

Chapter Thirteen

Being Business Minded (Part 3)

Change is coming to your Business!

In the previous Chapter, I made a comment, about what I called a "changing dispensation", and many of you were quite intrigued by this, and asked me to explain: Whenever I share a little story, my key objective is to help you extract one or two principles that you can apply when you find yourself in such a situation: For instance, I gave the story of Blackberry: Until they came along, our business model as a mobile network operator was to buy phones in bulk, as cheaply as possible, and sell them to our customers. Our business was not to sell phones but to get people to use them; our business was "airtime.". Now here was a new manufacturer (Blackberry) who did not want to just sell us phones but wanted a share of the airtime revenue—actually, they wanted the majority of the airtime revenue! I realised very quickly that they were not selling a phone, but a service. Blackberry is not a phone; it is a phone used to access the Internet. It was the first real "smartphone"" The game had changed!!....new dispensation! Companies like Nokia and Motorola, who had dominated the game until then, were in big, big trouble if they did not see this "change in dispensation"" Nokia failed to see this change and was taken to the cleaners. Giant companies like Ericsson's of Sweden and Siemens of Germany shut down their cell phone manufacturing businesses and fled at the coming of the "smartphone", boy"like Samsung and Apple! Others just became small-time players in an industry they had once dominated. "Changing dispensation." I also realised at that point that we would have to change quickly and turn our attention to things like mobile money services. Now we would have to hire bankers, insurance people, and even doctors (yes, we have medical doctors developing products). This was at a time when there was no Google, Twitter, Skype, Facebook, Alibaba, or WhatsApp. We would have to reach out to these new players and find ways to work with them, or get rolled over! Extract a principle now: It does not matter what industry you are in or how well-established it looks. Somewhere, somewhere, there is someone working on something that will completely turn it upside down! Uber is changing the public transport industry with taxis. Amazon took on the distribution of books. Netflix and similar services, will smash the traditional TV broadcasters, and Pay TV companies... Being business-minded means accepting this reality. It is something that should actually "excite" you. I get goose pimples...I love it! Another principle: In 1900, if a young man or woman, went to the most successful person around and said, "what business should I be in, to really be successful?", the answer would not be the same, when asked in 2000. And it would not be the same if asked in 2050. These are different dispensations: You should not be dreaming of being a rural bus operator! ... It is not a business of your dispensation. There are new industries being developed every day, at an ever-increasing pace.

Chapter Fourteen
Being Business Minded (Part 4)

Uber, EcoCash, or M-PESA are just the same! One of my young daughters, intrigued by what I said in my first chapter on being business-minded, asked me, "So how does a mobile money service, like EcoCash or M-PESA, actually work?" "It works just like Uber?" I replied. "How?" she asked, surprised. "Like Uber, they use a very sophisticated software platform to link up key partners in the transaction process. Uber relies on independent drivers, who own the cars and actually carry people. Our mobile money service, Ecocash, relies on thousands of independent small businesses that handle the actual transactions. If you think about it, the principles used in these two systems are exactly the same. Uber works, as a unique partnership, with the drivers... Mobile Money transfer systems, works as a unique partnership with thousands of small businesses." She stopped and reflected for a moment, then asked: "Do you think there are other partnerships, out there, that can use, this "Uber/Ecocash" type principle?" "The opportunities are actually limitless. You just have to be business-minded to find them. Why don't you think of other services that could be developed using the same principle?" Being business-minded is not just about creating new products or services; sometimes it is about bringing "disruptive" ideas to existing products and services. ......And if you come up with a great idea, be smart: don't go telling the whole world on Facebook, just do it!" In my next Chapter, I will tell you a remarkable story about a smart young lady, called Chido.. Who listened to me!

After Thought

There is a story told about a man who wanted to buy a Ferrari (a very expensive sports car) but was not happy about the delivery period for the car. He immediately went off and began to design his own car, and what he came up with is Ferrari's main competitor today: the Lamborghini. This did not happen simply because he had the money, but because he was "business-minded". A business-minded person is always thinking to themselves:

"Is there another way of doing this?

Or, can I come up with a better solution?"

Some of the greatest ventures have come when business-minded people see an opportunity in a bad service or bad product. "Consumer-minded" people just vent their anger. Before you rush off to complain, sit back and consider the opportunity for YOU!

Chapter Fifteen

Being Business Minded (Part 5)

"Witty inventions"

Proverbs 8:12 I wisdom dwell with prudence, and find out knowledge of witty inventions. Chido is one of my book fans; she reads every book I write and follows up with my "after thoughts," taking copious notes and extracting principles. One day she decided to visit her grandmother, who lived in a village about 400km from the capital city of her country, She would have to travel there by bus, or "catch a lift", from someone going to the area. The challenge for her was that the bus could be very intermittent and never really follow a particular schedule, and as for the "guys with lifts", she was afraid she might get someone who could harm her. Anyway, she would have to brave it, because that is the way it has always been. Only this time, as she sat in a rickety rural bus, she was thinking about something I had said in one of my Chapters: She was thinking about Uber. In her own research, she had discovered that the guy who set up Uber set it up because he could not get a taxi when he needed it: "Why can't we "Uber-ize" rural transport?"

she asked herself?: "Imagine, if I could get an SMS 30 minutes before the bus was getting close to my village, instead of waiting all day?" She had also read on the Internet about the "Uber car pool system," and she thought to herself, "If the guys who offer others a lift were on an "Uber-like" system, I would have a better chance of vetting who gives me a lift and when they are available." "Why doesn't some African entrepreneur come up with a system similar to Uber to solve our own transport problems? ... Surely, it must be possible to adapt the software they use for our challenges, here in Africa?" Returning from visiting her grandmother, Chido had to wait almost the whole day by the side of the road, trying to get a lift back to town. As usual, it was a harrowing experience for the young woman. Finally, she managed to squeeze herself into the back of a truck driven by a drunkard, who almost killed them. The following day she called a young friend, whom she often met at the Internet cafe, and she asked him a question: "James, you know how to write in code, don'" "I have Internet friends all over Africa and even as far as India who could help us develop something like this. Its actually not that difficult." James declared confidently.

The two of them reached out to some Internet friends, using social media, and began to develop their idea. Very soon they had a company, with partners in Nigeria, Kenya, India and America. ....when their company listed on the New York Stock Exchange, a few years later, they were richer than Aliko Dangote! Principle: Chido and James do not have to be imaginary characters. There are young people across the entire world who have the skills to solve this kind of problem, and many others like them. They do not need to buy buses to get into business, but they will end up making more money than any bus operator in history. They will be able to get into business with far less capital than I needed. Be "business conscious" or "business-minded." This is your dispensation!

After thought:

I did not have to share this vision with you. I could have implemented something like this within a few months. Someone out there will probably now run with it, and if you do, I hope you become a billionaire. I will not accuse you of "stealing" my idea, for the idea only belongs to those who are willing to take the risk and execute.

Nothing will give me greater joy than the day I hear that you made it with this or any similar idea.

The Lord said, "It is more blessed to give than to receive." So freely I give, as He commanded. The more ideas I give, the more I get. I'm now off to implement my next great idea.

Chapter Sixteen

Being Business Minded: So who is making the money? (Part 6)

A friend of mine, in South Africa, wanted me to join him, in acquiring a business called a "Breezing Farm". Something he said, intrigued me: "They have 50,000 cattle on one farm..." "Did you say 50,000 cattle?! Wow! I have never seen that many cattle in one place. I have to see this!" I exclaimed with excitement. Having walked around the farm and seeing all these cattle feeding in one place was pretty cool for a city slicker like me. "It would be great to have the bragging rights to saying, "I have 50,000 cattle!" I could just see how they would react back in my village." But before I got carried away, I had to look at the numbers. And when I look at numbers, I look at numbers. How do they make money, and how much? "Let me get this." I asked the Managing Director, of the operation: "You buy the cattle, from other farmers, and then you feed them. Then you sell them to the guy who slaughters them, and he sells them to the supermarkets?" "Yes". "Interesting." "So who makes the money?" "Its an industry.". "Tell me about this industry; I want to know everything about it." The management was professional and passionate about their business. It was clear they had been in it all their lives. Most of them had specialist agricultural degrees and MBAs. The more they spoke, the more I realized how sophisticated it all was. There is a science to everything: Now the guy was talking about the type of cattle they use, how they get the cattle to put on weight quickly, disease control, competitors from Brazil, etc. "Wow, they do that?!" "Yes, yes, yes." "I see". I wondered what the conversation with the professional farmer would have sounded like. Or, for that matter, the abattoir operator or the buyer at the supermarket chain. Respect. Respect. Being business-minded requires you to always approach things with humility and respect. There is nothing out there that is "simple.". Only fools look at what someone else is doing and say to themselves, "That is simple.". The process of reviewing their financial statements and business operations took me several months, working with industry consultants. It was harder than a telecommunications business. I decided not to buy the business, although I would have gladly invested for a minority stake, on condition that they stayed to run it. Understanding this distinction will prepare you for the "senior class" of business-minded people.

After thought 1.

"I want your advice. I have been approached by one of the largest computer companies in the world. They want me to be their partner. Its a great opportunity for me; those guys are global players." My friend said, hardly able to contain his excitement.

"Do you have a business plan for me to review?" I asked calmly.

"Don't you know who these guys are?! They are one of the biggest in the world. If they are interested, then they have done their homework. I must move quickly before I lose the opportunity."

"So what do you want from me?" I asked.

"Advice... And a small loan, to help me buy a stake."

"I'm sorry, I cannot help on either front."

The man was left bitter and angry. He sold his house and pursued his venture. Not long after, it went sour, and the big company never invested, but he lost all he had pursuing this "pipe dream.".

I know so many people who have failed in this way.

After thought 2.

There were two reasons I did not want to help the guy with the computer venture:

1. He wanted advice, but he had already made up his mind. Many people ask for "advice" on decisions they have already made. I do not advise such people!

2. The fact that you have been offered an opportunity by a big-named brand does not mean you do not have to do your homework and study the numbers properly. There are many people who rush to sell everything they have to get into an "opportunity," which they do not understand. To say "so and so is successful, so I will also be successful....is one of the roads to ruin.

Conclusion

Embracing the Dynamics of Change

As we come to an end of our investigation into the meaning of being "business minded," we consider a voyage characterized by tales of creativity, tenacity, and vision. Every chapter has revealed the key to handling change with skill and agility, from the early disruptions of the smartphone age to the revolutionary influence of mobile money services.

This series has shown how companies grow and fail not just because of their goods and services but also because of their capacity to foresee and adjust to "changing dispensations." Whether it was the revolutionary revenue-sharing model introduced by Blackberry or the emergence of game-changing apps like Uber and mobile money, one thing is certain: the business environment is always changing, necessitating constant attention to detail and a willingness to try new things.

Fundamentally, being "business minded" means adopting a mindset that views upheaval as a chance for development rather than just having strong financial judgment or strategic acumen. It's about taking lessons from other people's achievements and mistakes, distilling universal principles, and putting them to daring use in the pursuit of new projects and aspirations.

Keep the lessons weaved throughout these stories in mind as you set out on your own entrepreneurial path or work to improve your business skills. Aim to comprehend the processes of change, predict changes in the market, and cultivate an innovative culture in all that you do. By doing this, you not only put yourself in a position to prosper in the face of uncertainty but also make meaningful and significant contributions to the future of business.

www.ingramcontent.com/pod-product-compliance
Lightning Source LLC
Chambersburg PA
CBHW071952210526
45479CB00003B/908